HIRED!

NETWORKING TO LAND
THE JOB YOU WANT

Joel Abraham

authorHOUSE®

AuthorHouse™
1663 Liberty Drive
Bloomington, IN 47403
www.authorhouse.com
Phone: 1-800-839-8640

First published by AuthorHouse 4/18/2011

ISBN: 978-1-4567-4563-9 (e)
ISBN: 978-1-4567-4564-6 (sc)

Library of Congress Control Number: 2011905213

Printed in the United States of America

Any people depicted in stock imagery provided by Thinkstock are models,
and such images are being used for illustrative purposes only.
Certain stock imagery © Thinkstock.

This book is printed on acid-free paper.

Because of the dynamic nature of the Internet, any web addresses or
links contained in this book may have changed since publication and
may no longer be valid. The views expressed in this work are solely those
of the author and do not necessarily reflect the views of the publisher,
and the publisher hereby disclaims any responsibility for them.

Contents

Special Thanks

I would like to thank everyone who helped turn my dream of writing a book into reality. Being dyslexic, I never thought I would ever write a book. Writing has always been my nemesis, one I have been aggressively fighting for the past 30 years.

This book would not have been possible without the brutal honesty of the countless job seekers, mentors and clients I have networked with on a daily basis over the past 17 years. I also would like to thank my wife, Kathy, and my parents for motivating me to do the most difficult thing first throughout my life. And finally, I would like to thank Andi for pushing me into action by proofreading this book with patience and thoughtful insight.

Thank you all for everything.

Joel

Dedication

"Boundaryless people, excited by speed and inspired by stretch dreams, have an absolutely infinite capacity to improve everything."

From the Files of Jack Welch © 2003 by The McGraw-Hill Companies Inc,

I am dedicating this life changing guide to all the "boundaryless" job seekers who feel trapped in the tradition of waiting for opportunities. I have helped network thousands of people for the last 17 years. I am confident that by using the tips and tools presented in this book you will be able to liberate yourself from your job search and take control of your network. Your network will not only uncover opportunities for you and others, but give you the confidence that you need to surpass any peak or valley during the job search process.

The premise of this information is to help you create a career plan and avoid major pitfalls or common areas of challenge. I will share tips and techniques to enhance your resume. I will also examine how prepare for the job interview, build a sustainable network and socially engineer networking encounters that will help you break through the walls of the job "black hole."

You will see that (second to effort) your state of mind is the most important element throughout this journey. When you start reading this guide, you will have begun the journey of running yourself like your own business. This guide will give you actionable practices that will help you shape your future — your future of independence.

We have learned from this recession that you can no longer be caught off guard. We all have families, bills to pay and other obligations. As a result, I refuse to (not be) prepared; especially knowing that I can lose my job at any time. It is my hope that through the tips and techniques presented in this book, I can help you also be prepared, and never be caught off guard.

I remember clearly the first time I got laid off. This one crucial moment started my personal journey to find the best method to help me save time, and grow a sustainable network that could help me in my job search. I knew that establishing an effective network could proactively and selfishly create my pipeline of opportunities. More important, I could use my network to not be selfish, and "pay it forward."

Helping others is extremely important. Many use social networking as a way to build a pipeline of personal job opportunities to help themselves only. While networking, your reputation is all you have. You have to be honest. Honesty helps you create strong healthy networks that bring in business opportunities, create new partnerships and new pathways into innovative industries. In this book, we will discuss social networking etiquette, and I will give you examples of how I have used technology to strike up conversations that have helped take the awkwardness out of many first connections.

I have seen more unemployed top talent in the last two

years than in the entire span of my career as a recruiter, (which includes two other recessions). I knew that I could do something to help. I have been able to assist many job seekers with this information, and you will read quotes directly from them. You will read stories about how minor changes in their job search process attracted job opportunities quicker than before. They now had options — no longer did they feel trapped by applying for jobs and waiting endlessly for recruiters to respond.

I caution all who read and apply the techniques presented in this book that searching for the right job takes effort. Landing the job *you* want is not a marathon a race. You still have to use traditional sources. If you are not mentally ready, or do not have the time to put forth the effort, I urge you to wait until you are. To those who are ready, I hope you will find new creative ways to differentiate yourself and locate the opportunities to build a sustainable social network that you and others can draw from at anytime.

I appreciate the opportunity to share my thoughts and experience with you. It is my wish that you find at least one piece of information, or useful tip that helps make a difference in your life. All I ask is that you pay it forward by helping other job seekers who feel the same way you did before embarking on this job search journey. Please know that I am proud of the effort you are putting forth right now to achieve your goals.

Have a fruitful job search.

Foreword

HIRED! Networking to Land the Job YOU Want

I want to share with you why I chose this title for the book. For the past three years there have been two common complaints I hear most from job seekers. First, job seekers are tired of not getting any feedback from recruiters. If they do, all they get is the same canned e-mail or letter response: "thanks, but no thanks. It's not you, it's me."

The second biggest complaint I hear is about the job "black hole." Job seekers on a daily basis are spending time submitting countless resumes, filling out online applications and customizing cover letters while not receiving any feedback from an employer. Most job seekers are coming to the realization that they are wasting their time working through a company's website and job board. The results of their effort in terms of time and money are causing depression and major blows to the candidate's self-esteem.

> "I agree that submitting countless numbers of resumes to company websites seems pointless. I would much rather speak with an actual person in human resources than wait for an automated response." *Graduate student at Monmouth University*

"With most ads generating up to 700 candidates, it's an employer's market. After about hundreds of resumes and applications without a response, I gave up blindly applying to posted ads three months ago. With an impending military deployment, I stopped applying to jobs altogether. Hopefully the job market will get better when I get back." *Health-care manager*

"The biggest challenge is getting the opportunity to speak with *anyone* responsible for hiring. How do you get to the point of even an informational interview? There is indeed a lack of responsiveness on the part of prospective employers. A short e-mail would be nice. I've e-mailed back after phone calls or applications and, then, nothing." *Freelance writer*

This is the reason why I wrote this book. To give you, the job seeker, the ability to differentiate yourself so that you can proactively get connected to influencers, get a live conversation that will help you land the job you want. Also, the ability to build a sustainable network that will attract new opportunities for you.

Some of the techniques I am sharing are viewed as *social engineering*. For most people, this is a new term for an old concept. Hence, I would like to define the term *social engineering*, and explain how I apply this concept during a job search.

Leveraging Your Network for Jobs and Opportunities

I define *social engineering* as the act of proactively leveraging all aspects of human interaction during a job search in an honest and ethical manner. Social engineering techniques include:

- Assertively using social networks to uncover the right contacts for jobs to which you have not had any exposure;

- Using your network to uncover and identify opportunities before they are made public; and

- Communicating strategies that build a long, lasting network of referrals and contacts that will benefit you now and into the future.

The information and tactics I am going to share have liberated job seekers from the traditional "wait-and-see" or the job "black hole" of not obtaining any feedback from an employers. I am confident that if these techniques are applied without honesty or that if you embellish your skills, you will be discovered quickly and your networks will dry up and shrivel away. However, if you have a positive attitude, are trustworthy, and resourceful then you will build long-lasting relationships that will consistently deliver opportunities to you and others in your network.

About Me

For more than 17 years, I have been recruiting decision-makers in the information technology (IT), security, biotechnology, retail, health care, manufacturing, and life sciences industries across the United and Canada. I have competed with hundreds of agencies, integrators and consulting companies. I have interviewed thousands of candidates. I started my career in 1993, during a recession, and I made it through the Internet boom and subsequent bust. Today I find myself coming out of my third recession during my staffing tenure. One thing I have learned in my career as a recruiter is that the market is constantly changing and you cannot control the direction in which it changes. However, you *can* take ownership of your career.

The first time I got laid off made me realize I had to take ownership of my career. Luckily, I was unemployed for only one day thanks to my professional contacts and social networks.

Usually, when I tell people that they have control over their career, I typically hear:

"Yeah right, I cannot control whether or not I receive a pink slip or if my company goes out of business."

My response to that statement is simply you are WRONG! It is interesting to see the look on people's faces when I say that. People typically pause, and I then proceed to share with them that they do indeed have control. I remind them that they need to run themselves like their own business.

What do I mean by running yourself like a business? Simple — you need to have a plan or roadmap. You have to set personal and professional goals, both short and long term, and network to make sure you have influential contacts. You must understand what the variance is between where you are right now, and where you would like to be both personally and professionally.

Most people are reactive instead of proactive. And with the economy going south, they are like deer caught in the headlights. They have no existing network, and are forced to work with staffing companies. One of the biggest mistakes people make is to panic. I understand this mindset; I have been laid off too. As a result, they send their resumes to hundreds of random agencies, or quickly put together a resume without taking stock of the content.

The unintentional consequence is that when you become one of many people fighting for that one spot, it becomes increasingly difficult to separate yourself from the top 20 percent of candidates applying to get the job you want. It is my intention to give you the tools, techniques and confidence to assertively go out in your industry and create a sustainable network that will bring multiple opportunities to you, instead of sitting and waiting for a job. I realized this when I was speaking at my first job camp, which was the catalyst for this guide.

"THE DEFINITION OF INSANITY IS DOING THE SAME THING OVER AND OVER AGAIN AND EXPECTING DIFFERENT RESULTS." ALBERT EINSTEIN

Job Camp Experience Leading to This Journey

I attended my first job camp as a speaker to share career tips with all different types of job seekers. The job camp provided some really unique forums, such as creating and delivering your elevator pitch, writing your resume and teaching attendees how to use the Internet to grow a social network. I saw an army of volunteers ready to help people craft and review their resumes. There were also many speakers and roundtable discussions. My job for this event was to discuss with people how to differentiate themselves through their own accomplishments, and help them proactively build networks that will bring them new opportunities.

I quickly found my roundtable. People slowly came in and sat down. As I looked around, attendees looked shy and uncomfortable. At first glance, I could see they were from the X and Y generations. I was given less than 20 minutes to help as many people as I could Because I could not waste any time, I quickly persuaded 15 nearby attendees to join the discussion. I love my job, and my goal was to help as many people as possible in those 20 minutes.

The group comprised of Baby Boomers and Generation X and Y attendees. Before starting, I asked people to raise their hands if they were looking for work. Everyone raised their hands. I then asked how many were currently working and scared about their current job situation. One person dropped her hand. I then proceeded to ask the group how many people had been laid off for a month or less. One person's hand came down. I asked the same question, but using a three-month period. Three hands dropped. Lastly, I used the time frame of more than one year and the rest of the hands came down. Basically, more than 65 percent of the job seekers at my table had been looking for a job for more than a year.

Although I was shocked, reality set in quickly. I saw the same haunting stares from the many job seekers I had helped in the past who were desperate for a job to pay their bills. I saw the angry job seeker, the shocked and the recently laid-off job seeker. It was the hardened job seeker I could relate to most because of my experience with past recessions. I could see the battle scars obtained from fighting for those few coveted jobs, in a volatile economy, with a 16.7 percent unemployment rate.

I introduced myself and asked a few questions on how people look for a job. I then asked attendees to explain what they hated the most about the job search process. Everyone agreed it was applying for a job and waiting for feedback.

And they were right. Traditional job hunting methods are one dimensional. You apply and wait, several times, and don't get any feedback. Waiting erodes your confidence, which leads to ugly thoughts and self-doubt.

To land the job you want in today's job hunting market you have to be multi-dimensional. You must use all of the tools available to you: apply online, use job boards, contact staffing and out-placement firms. All of these tools make up a balanced and well-rounded job hunting plan.

I knew I had to break through to the skeptics, and be taken seriously. Consequently, I shared with them the most important tip that changed everyone's outlook and the course of our discussion that day.

Business Challenge + Your Solution = Accomplishment™

The strategy leading to the most positive change for the job seekers attending my table was using the Formula for Accomplishments. This formula enables job seekers to create true accomplishments that differentiate the job seeker from their competition. The formula is simple:

Once I shared the formula, the whole group woke up. I asked for a resume. The first one I got was a professional, one-page resume on card stock. This job seeker was a Baby Boomer who has been laid off for six months. I took a quick glance at his resume and nothing stood out. All I saw was a list of his responsibilities, which blended in together. If I were looking at 10 resumes, I would have tossed it aside.

After glancing at his resume, I shared with him that his content was well written and his responsibilities were solid. However, there was nothing that would differentiate him from someone else. I asked him how long he had been working at his last job. "A long time," he replied. I then asked him to share with us one problem he solved he felt proud of. He shared with the table that he was able to improve the payment speed to vendors, thus securing the rate of distribution to clients.

I then told him to dig deeper. "What was the problem?" I asked. He said that the company was able to pay faster and keep their suppliers happy. "That's great," I said, "but what would have been the impact if the suppliers were not happy and there were issues with the distribution?" He told me that the distribution problems they were having affected their largest client and that their client was unhappy about their reliability. He then realized what I was trying to do:

Business Challenge + Your Solution = Accomplishments ™

- <u>Challenge</u>: Customer service issues that resulted from distribution issues.

- <u>Solution:</u> Program created to pay suppliers faster, thus ensuring priority distribution.

- <u>Accomplishment</u>: Client satisfied and sales increased.

This job seeker identified distribution issues that impacted the client. Furthermore, he developed a process that paid the vendors faster to ensure priority distribution. The result was a satisfied customer and increased profitability.

Nearly instantaneously the formula resonated with most folks sitting at the table. I started to hear a flurry of questions wondering how this could be applicable if their role was not tied to dollars. One of the X generation job seeker asked me if company awards are considered an accomplishment. I asked him what he meant by that. He began to tell me that at his previous place of employment he made a video advertisement for a client. The client and his peers loved it so much that they recognized him with a company award that was not financial in nature.

I proceeded to ask him why he won the award. "Because of the creative way I shot the video," he said. "This is great, but, what did the customer think?" I asked. He said that the customer liked it and televised the video. He then smiled and said, "I understand where you are going with this." "The formula for an accomplishment is Business Challenge + Your Solution = Accomplishments," I emphasized. Everyone at the roundtable laughed. They now understood the formula and its basic concept.

Because we were running out of time, I changed gears to talk about the dreaded salary question and how to respond to it.

Here is what I teach people to say:

> "There are two reasons why I am here today. First, money is important. But second, and most important,

is opportunity. I see a lot of opportunity here at ABC Company, and because of this opportunity I do not want to price myself out of this position. Therefore, I would entertain your strongest offer."

I learned this through a recruitment master by the name of Peter Leffkowitz. Most likely, the hiring manager or recruiter will not have experienced this objection. You will still have to tell them what you are making in salary, including incentives and benefits. But you have just created a common ground letting them know that you are willing to take a short-term loss for a long-term gain. The company now has the ability to do the same.

I reminded them that this is where people sink, swim or get removed from the hiring process all together. As a recruiter, I understand that you do not want to sell yourself short, or price yourself out of an opportunity. However, if the job seeker does not answer this question, the recruiter will not feel they have control over their candidate. Moreover, if the company is not sure they can afford you, they will not pursue you. Employers do not want to waste their time or put themselves in a situation that has a bad ending for all parties.

Attendees were not accepting my response to the salary question. So I shared with them a story about a conversation I had from a well-respected executive. This professional saw a job that he thought was a perfect fit for him. I found him the name of the human resources contact to whom he reached out directly. After applying to the job online, he waited for a response for two weeks, and he got nothing. He called me for feedback. However, the entire conversation centered on all the reasons he thought caused him not to get any feedback.

"I'm too old, too experienced, too expensive" and tons more, he explained. I asked him a simple question; "Did you talk to the human resources contact?" "No," he laughed and said. "Then how do you know all of this information?" I asked. He said nothing. "Can you control this?" I followed. "No," he said. I asked a third question, "What can you control then?" "Networking and proactively seeking opportunities," he replied. "If you really want this job use LinkedIn and your contacts to move up the food chain and build relationships," I said.

The table was quiet. I told them it was time for them to take control of their future. We discussed how LinkedIn can provide them with the ability to network and find contacts in their industry, or companies that they want to learn more about. I shared with them the etiquette, how to prioritize their connections, create a communication plan, and finally, to not be the networker who only calls when they need something.

This proactive approach will not only build confidence, but will help you get the "job search monkey" off your back. Now, you can say to yourself, "my job search is in progress and I have spoken to five, six or 10 people this week." I reminded roundtable attendees that this is a marathon and not a short-distance race. If you want to free yourself from the job waiting game, you need to network. Networking will attract opportunities to you. How do you think job seekers land an opportunity prior to it being posted in a job board?

As I looked around the tables, I immediately saw the motivated job seekers who got it, and would put forth the effort into making this change. Also there were the few job seekers who were not mentally ready for the commitment. It saddens me a bit to see this time and again.

The last thing discussed on this topic was that attitude and/ or state of mind is 99 percent of the battle. Therefore, if you are starting to think unfounded negative thoughts, you must immediately let them go from your brain. You must simply focus on what you can control to find your opportunity.

After the discussion was over I walked around the event, observed different stations and how hard and selfless the volunteers looked. Most people I saw that day were working hard trying to improve themselves. I walked into one of the presentations and there must have been hundreds of people taking notes. I listened to one speaker talk about what a good resume should look like and how to share the story of your career.

Why am I sharing this with you? What I saw was Einstein's definition of insanity. These job seekers were using and being taught the same old traditional apply-and-wait job hunting tactics. And these tactics were baring no fruit for months or, worse, years. This book will show you proactive techniques that will give you the confidence you need during your job search and explain nontraditional ways to leverage your network to land the job you want in a shorter period of time regardless of the current economic climate.

I realized later that night I had the experience to help others find a job. I felt compelled to write this book to help those motivated job seekers who want to take back control of their lives in this uncertain economic time. The information I am going to expand on and share I believe will work in any job peak or valley.

Creating a Sustainable Career Plan

This is where your career plan starts to form and take shape. You have to identify where you are right now in your professional life and where you would like to be. I know this process is a gut-check for most, especially for those who are under- or unemployed. This information is critical for you as you build a sustainable network and plan.

A career plan is no different than a map. You can either get to where you want to be by winging it or get a map to arrive at your destination faster.

The Career Map

The plan is your map. As in life, sometimes you hit road blocks, make mistakes or have accidents. When this happens to you during your career search, you have to adjust and continue on your mission with the same plan.

Drafting an effective career plan takes careful thought and planning, in addition to networking and understanding your position in the current employment market. When attempting to understand where you stand in the current job market, consider these four points:

- The current unemployment rate is 20 percent across the United States, including the disenfranchised or people who have given up looking for work.

- Seventy-five percent of the employment population would consider a new opportunity if they were called. *(How to Get Ready for a Surge in Replacement Hiring" by Lou Adler)*

- The result of this mass flood of talent to the candidate marketplace is frustration, wage reductions, uncertainty and fierce competition for available openings.

- Employers are facing the same frustration. Even though wages have dropped, the number of unqualified resumes and interviews are taking up valuable time employers simply do not have.

Given everything you are going through personally and professionally, how or where do you start? First, you need to know your market value. This, in my opinion, is the hardest phase of building your career plan because you have to uncover your most vulnerable thoughts and realities. However, once you bull through this part, not only will your confidence grow, but you will realize the rest of your plan is based solely on the effort you put in. Please note that I am not downplaying effort — effort is the key to success.

With that said, let's find out what your current market value is.

Your Market Value

> **Current Situation.** *To determine your market value, you need to answer seven tough questions:*

1. Where am I at financially?

2. What mistakes can I correct from my past careers?

3. How prepared was I to face the current recession?

4. What is my competitive advantage to the market place?

5. What lessons have I learn during this last or any previous recessions?

6. Am I willing to take a short-term loss for a long-term gain?

7. What are my geographic and travel options? Willing to relocate?

But once you answer these questions you can move forward with a clear idea of what risks you are willing to or can take, what your desired compensation is, whether you are willing to relocate and your financial obligations are.

Salary Setting a Competitive Compensation. This is a personal area, and the answers to the questions you have asked yourself will help you to determine what you need, want and will accept. The salary you choose is up to you. I can only give you the ability to answer the questions properly so that you do not price yourself out of the job you are targeting. Refer to the "Avoiding Common Pitfalls" section on how to answer the dreaded salary question below.

Setting a Contract Rate. If you are looking for contracting work or looking to establish an LLC or S-Corp, you should talk to an accountant to make sure you incorporate properly and price yourself from an expense standpoint. This will include such benefits as vacation, personal leave time, retirement and bonuses, among others.

Overall, clients will dictate what rates they can afford. Most of the time, you are not going to know what that final rate if you are working with staffing company or integrator. Remember, they are in the business to make money too. Their job is to negotiate the most favorable rate to keep you competitive and to make as much money as they can. Supply and demand for specific skills plays a major role in this process. You should keep abreast of the needs for your particular skill by using tools like Indeed.com or job boards to keep track of current trends in your industry.

Duration of the assignment is also a factor. It is reasonable to ask for a higher rate for shorter-term contracts and a lower rate for longer-term contracts.

Consider the following factors when determining your rate:

- If you have worked as a contractor before, what was your rate on previous, similar contracts?

- Does the new project involve more business experience combined with more responsibility or management?

- Is this position on call or are you going to have to put more than 40 hours in a week to hit project deadlines?

- Last, and most important, how competitive is the market for your skills? This is where you are going to have to educate yourself on what is happening in the industry so you do not price yourself out of this opportunity.

Most salary websites, in my experience, inflate salaries by 10 percent to 15 percent. Therefore, you need to check multiple sources if you use this as a way to check your market value. Also, use your network to see what others are being paid for contract work. Most contractors are willing to help as long as you are not competing for the same opportunity.

Finally, as in any good negotiation, you will need to establish two real rates: your ideal rate and the walk-away rate (i.e. where this opportunity does not become profitable for you). Every time you talk to a recruiter you need to keep those two numbers in the back of your mind.

Traditional Job Hunting Processes

Most of the people I talk to on a daily basis about their resume are just like the candidate depicted in the conversation you will read below.

- Me: "What is the objective or goal of your resume?"

- Candidate: "To get a job opportunity that will enable me to show the employer I meet the job qualifications and land an interview. Here is what I have done in my background. Here is what I have accomplished. Here is why I should be the preferred candidate."

- Me: "Have you worded your resume to fit what the company is looking for?"

- Candidate: "Correct."

- Me: "What in this resume differentiates you from everyone else?"

- Candidate: "Good question. The resume may not exhibit that. I try to get into the greater details of my background and customize the cover letter to meet the company's needs."

The candidate then explained his background is different because he has combined skills in operations, technology and management. Most candidates usually do a good job of pitching their skills and responsibilities. When he was finished, I asked him if what he described for me were responsibilities.

- Candidate: "That's correct."
- Me: "Do you think that separates you from your competitors?"
- Candidate:"No."

At this point, I always share with candidates that there is a distinct difference between responsibilities and accomplishments. When I looked at his resume, I saw little to no content in his resume that showed the true business impact he made or that would give resume screeners any information that would make them to pick up the phone and call the candidate for an interview.

I asked the candidate to describe an accomplishment in his most recent job of which he was proud. He shared with me that the company had major business process problems that created a five-year backlog of issues. That caused the company to set aside significant dollars to resolve the issue that were originally slated for other strategic projects. He told me that he developed solutions that resolved the problems in less than six months, freeing up the money that was originally slated for strategic initiatives that would allow the company to increase its competitive advantage.

I then shared with him the Formula for Accomplishments (Business Challenge + Your Solution = Accomplishments), and he immediately got excited because he now realized how to craft his competitive advantages. He realized that he saw a business deficiency and created a solution that resulted in an accomplishment. This always resonates with any interviewer.

Accomplishments give the resume screener an emotional connection to a specific event. This connection stems from the fact that most businesses face the same challenges no matter the industry sector. The interviewer may not be able to relate to a candidate's job or industry experience, but she will relate to common business issues that are faced by all companies. Accomplishments also demonstrate candidates' business acumen, their ability to identify business challenges and their problem solving skills.

All of a sudden, our dialogue got livelier and I saw the confidence growing along with his energy level. "It is important for you to take a step back and look at your job from a 10,000-foot view," I added. "This will enable you to actually see where you fit in the company." For instance, how did his role impact the business? Who were his clients, and how would they be impacted by him solving these issues or, more important, if he was not able to solve those issues?

I strongly encourage you to review your resume and identify if it truly differentiates you from other potential candidates. Doing so will enable you to start changing your thought process from that of a traditional resume to one that includes true differentiators that make you unique.

Resume

Crafting the right resume is the first step in running yourself like a business. You can compare this process to writing an executive summary for a business plan. The first step is to realize that businesses do not care about what you do between the hours of 9 a.m. to 5 p.m. This is not to say that you shouldn't put your responsibilities on your resume. What I am saying is that the key to standing out among the masses are your accomplishments, no matter how big or small.

I usually get asked, "What are meaningful accomplishments?" Think about how you saved the company money, reduced time, increased workflow and improved the quality of life for your internal or external customers. This might be something as simple as creating an Excel spreadsheet that saved everybody at work time or something as extraordinary as closing a $10 million deal.

Now you ask, "What should my resume look like?" This is where it gets tricky because resume format are a matter of personal taste. In addition, you will get different advice from recruiters, human resources professionals and out-placement companies. Following are my recommendations for organizing a resume.

Customized Look:

This is a topic that I get a lot of questions regarding. How should a resume look and feel? What paper color and font size should you use? The style and flair of your resume is up to you. What I am concerned about is the content and structure of resume. The only thing I am going to add here is that if you have more than 10 years of experience, your resume should tell your story.

It is okay for a resume to be longer than two pages, but it should not be book. For example, a resume for a technologist will be much longer and should describe your work and the technologies with which you have work. My advice is to keep it under five to seven pages of good, relevant content. If you have five to seven pages of pontifications, your audience will toss your resume.

Structure:

The structure of your resume is important. I have seen common and avoidable pitfalls that have affected the ability of some job seekers to be found or that have ranked them lower on search strings because of missing information.

Embedded Contact Information

Do not to write your contact information in headers or footers. I have received hundreds of resumes throughout the past five years with embedded contact information. Why is this a resume pitfall? Because some applicant tracking systems that import your resume are not able to strip the data out a header or footer. The result is a resume with no contact information. Why take the risk?

Missing Critical Key Words

This is an important area for any resume regardless of job type and industry. You need to make sure that the skills listed in your resume can be searchable keywords. This will enable your resume to show up in the top 20 percent of searches performed via an applicant tracking system or job board.

I am going to use sales as an example. Let's say a company is looking for an outside sales representative that knows Microsoft Word and sales technology such as Salesforce.com. However, you assume that everyone knows Word and do not write this in your resume. The result is that all of the candidates listing all three keywords separately will rank higher than you during the job search. If your market is competitive with a lot of job seekers, the employer may only look at the first 10 candidates. Thus, you may not be one of them because you did not put that in your resume.

Important tip: you need to be honest when writing the different technology applications you are familiar with or know how to use. If you state that you know how to use a particular software and do not know how to use it you will lose all credibility during the interview process once you are found out. In today's market, the word *knowledgeable* in a resume has been tarnished by people who do not have actual experience and will most likely be grilled with interview questions. So if you are not comfortable with the technology or skill, do not list it on your resume.

Recruitment and Job Seeking Technologies

This is a key factor. It is important for you to show what technologies you are comfortable using. I have seen situations in which Biotechnology companies are requiring the CEOs to sit down and demonstrate their ability to use PowerPoint.

Most recruitment searches are based on software applications that use keywords and Boolean queries to find the top resumes that fit the company's needs. Some applicant tracking systems have ranking tools that filter and measure job key words versus the resume's keywords. The same holds true for job boards, social networks and search engines.

Key: Make sure you add a technology section at the bottom of your resume that has all of the software application and technologies you are functional in including, Word, Excel, PowerPoint and the like. Do not assume everyone knows how to use PowerPoint.

Objectives

What do you want from a company? If you get what you want, how are you going to contribute? What will be the result of your contribution? For example: *I am looking for a progressive, team-oriented company in which I can use my X skills and experience to contribute to overall to the overall profitability or productivity of Company/Team.*

Experience

My advice for you here is to be detailed with your company, job titles and dates. If you do not add dates, they will toss your resume. (this is not finite, it's a likely outcome but not certain)

Education

If you are a college, or associate graduate, and do not have any practical experience in your field, you may want to list your education before your professional experience. The same holds true for your affiliations, such as associations and charitable institutions you may work with on a volunteer basis.

References Available Upon Request

Some recruiters may use references as leads for new customers or candidates. Therefore, only provide references if requested.

Formula for Accomplishments

Business Challenge + Your Solution
= Accomplishments™

In today's uncertain economy, the competition for the top jobs is getting fierce. Most people ask me what they can do to their resumes to stand out from the masses. My answer is inevitably the same. What are your accomplishments?

Most people get frustrated when I ask them to sell me on themselves or tell me what some of their accomplishments have been. They tell me they can't think of any now or have not done anything that has saved the company millions of dollars. This only tells me that they are too close to their jobs and do not know how to identify what an accomplishment is and more important, how to share an accomplishment to show their business acumen.

Being dyslexic, I looked at this process backwards for myself. I noticed that most companies have the same goals or similar problems, whether they are in the service or manufacturing industry — that is, companies want to make a profit, reduce costs, improve customer service, etc.

Resume after resume, I see bullet points or simple sentences like, "I saved the company $500 or increased sales by 38 percent." While this might a great accomplishment, from an outsider's perspective, I do not know if $500 is a lot or a little. I also don't know how your accomplishment, as worded, impacted the company's bottom line, if at all. Lots of questions and assumptions are left up to whoever is reading your resume and your whole professional story was not told.

Using the Formula for Accomplishments will allow you to identify how your work added value to the organization, and tell this vital piece of importance to prospective employers or recruiters.

Business Challenge + Your Solution = Accomplishment™

As stated earlier, organizations face the same challenges. For example:

- Make money.
- Save money.
- Reduce cost.
- Improve customer service.
- Improve employee morale.
- Enhance communication across the organization.

They key to this formula is that accomplishments never change. What did change were the business challenges you faced, what your recommended solutions were and the result of that solution. (Warning: Accomplishments should be no longer than three to four lines. You are not writing a dissertation.)

Writing an accomplishment using this formula will demonstrate you business intelligence, and the person reading the resume will be able to relate to your challenges company. In addition, you will have given the recruiter or human resources professional marketing information to sell your background to their internal or external customer.

Use the spaces below to craft your own accomplishments using the Formula for Accomplishments:

Business Challenge + Your Solution = Accomplishment™

_____

_____

_____

_____

Resume Accomplishment Examples

While I attended the job camp, I heard from a lot of people working in different industries how in their line of work they did not work on projects that could equate to an accomplishment. Regardless of your industry, or job, everyone has accomplishments that impact their business or employer.

Here are some examples:

Bar and Restaurant

Before Using the Formula for Accomplishments

Bar/Restaurant, City, State   Sr. Waitress
Month Year to Present

Serve alcoholic beverages and small amounts of food to customers. Maintaining clean work environment. Achieving sales quotas. Training new waitresses.

Accomplishments: Implemented a new training program to decrease turnover rate. Hit sales bonus on a regular basis while also training. Served as liaison between management and waitresses. Created new training manual. Created promotional materials

After Applying Formula for Accomplishments

Bar/Restaurant, City, State   Sr. Waitress
Month Year to Present

Accomplishments: Bar/Restaurant had significant staff turnover and sales goals were consistently missed. I created and implemented a staff training program with incentives and promotional events. As a result, staff turnover was reduced by more than 50 percent, which improved overall customer satisfaction and lead to hitting sales quotas consistently.

New Collage Graduate

Before Using the Formula for Accomplishments

Company ABC, City, State
Editing Internship   Month Year–Month Year

- Edited client reports for quality and content.

- Worked with professional editors to gain feedback.

- Translated documents from American English to British Standard English.

- Performed with a high degree of accuracy.

- Effectively prioritized work to meet deadlines.

After Applying Formula for Accomplishments

Company ABC, City, State
Editing Internship   Month Year–Month Year

Company Definition: Company X is a consulting firm that provides customized talent assessment, succession planning strategies, leadership development and executive coaching. Company X consultants apply industrial organization psychology to research and create flexible human capital assessment services for customers. This gives client's the ability to make educated hiring and promotional decisions that result in a positive impact on their organization.

Accomplishments: Translation inconsistencies created quality issues due to time constraints. I provided the experience, expertise and process to resolve those issues. As a result, international clients received an improved product in a shorter period of time that improved their ability to hire at the speed of their business.

Teaching

Before Using the Formula for Accomplishments

School City, State   **Advanced Placement**
Chemistry Teacher   **Year – Present**

Accomplishments:

- Designed and implemented college-level chemistry curriculum.

- Enhanced critical thinking and high-level problem solving skills in students.

- Promoted self-motivation and college-level study skills for students.

- Developed laboratory investigations following college-board recommendations.

- Worked after school hours with students individually or in small groups.

- Maintained the chemistry stockroom for the department – managed inventory and the ordering of chemicals, equipment and other supplies.

After Appying Formula for Accomplishments

School City, State **Advanced Placement**
Chemistry Teacher **Year – Present**

Accomplishments: The tenured advanced placement (AP) chemistry teacher passed away unexpectedly leaving a major gap in the science department. During my first year as the AP chemistry teacher, I developed and implemented an aggressive chemistry curriculum designed to challenge high-functioning students. The results were 76 percent of my students (13 out of 17) received a passing score (3 or higher) on the AP chemistry exam.

Nonprofit

Before Using the Formula for Accomplishments

Organization, City, State **Case Worker**
Month Year to Present

Accomplishments:

- Motivate and involve parents on the education of their children.

- Encourage and mentor homeless and at-risk children, reinforcing positive behavior.

- Teach and relate natural and spiritual principles to children and provide job skills, clothing and resources for low-income families

- Collect appropriate information to assess client needs and create and implement social programs for the community.

- Compile, audit and analyze business information and approve advertisement for social and other programs.

- Conduct weekly follow-up home visits and provide written progress reports.

After Applying Formula for Accomplishments

Organization, City, State   Case Worker
Month Year to Present

Accomplishments: New nonprofit organization did not have the proper qualification. I coordinated, organized and established the organization's 501(c)(3) tax-exempt status with the Internal Revenue Service. The result was a stronger brand for the charity by creating successful Toys for Tots and back to school programs, which improved the quality of life for disadvantaged children in the community.

Mid-technical

Before Using the Formula for Accomplishments

Company ABC, City, State   Project Manager-
Assembly & Shipping   Year to Present

Working as Project Manager for our Assembling and Shipping department, I was responsible for organizing the assembling, shipping and receiving activities of the company.

Accomplishments:

- Researched the existing system to understand the various pain points with project sponsors.

- Developed business case and high-level scope to identify various tasks to improve the existing manual system and a new automated system.

- Worked with subject-matter experts to develop

project plans and a work breakdown structure of the projects.

- Consolidated lessons learned and maintained documents for future use. Key stakeholders were always kept informed on the status of the projects.

After Applying Formula for Accomplishments

Company ABC, City, State   Project Manager-
Assembly & Shipping   Year to Present

Accomplishments: Customer service issues were rampant due a manual assembling process. I developed a new, repeatable, automated system process that was customizable to solve our client's pain points, resulting in improved client retention, overall satisfaction and an increase in project profitability for the company.

Military

Before Using the Formula for Accomplishments

U.S. Army, City, State   Cable Team NCO
Month Year to Present

Accomplishments:

- Installed, maintained, repaired and modified copper, coaxial and fiber-optic cable systems.

- Used engineered drawings, work statements and technical manuals to determine requirements for underground and buried cable systems.

- Prepared and installed distribution equipment.

- Terminated tip cables on main distribution frames.

- Ensured techniques, materials and accomplishments according to technical standards, specifications and engineering directives.

- Performed pneumatic troubleshooting to locate faulty splice cases and pressure component assemblies, using resistance measurements and pressure gradients.

After Applying Formula for Accomplishments

U.S. Army, City, State Cable Team NCO
Month Year to Present

Accomplishments: Failing to deploy communication equipment on the battle field is not an option. I assisted in the planning and execution of innovative tactics that ensured success for our missions and soldiers in the field. As a result, I was awarded the Meritorious Service Medal.

Use the spaces below to craft your own accomplishments using the Formula for Accomplishments:

Business Challenge + Your Solution = Accomplishment™

_____

_____

_____

_____

Business Challenge + Your Solution = Accomplishment™

_____

_____

_____

_____

Business Challenge + Your Solution = Accomplishment™

_____

_____

_____

_____

Resume Format Using the Formula for Accomplishments

CANDIDATE NAME, CERTIFICATIONS

Address • City, State and Zip •
(111) 111-1111 (home) • (222) 222-2222 (cell) • E-mail

PROFILE

Senior-level IT executive seeking a position that leverages my leadership qualities and proven technical and communications skills to provide business-focused services adhering to regulatory controls.

PROFESSIONAL EXPERIENCE

Company City, State   **Month Year – Present**

Company Definition: name is a leader in the financial management sector, providing financial and accounting management services to public and private organizations in commercial markets throughout the United States.

Title, Security and Risk Executive

> **Accomplishments**

-
-

> **Responsibilities**

-
-
-
-

2nd Position Title

> **Accomplishments**

-
-

> **Responsibilities**

-
-
-
-

Company City, State   **Month Year – Present**

Company Definition: name is a leader in the financial management sector, providing financial and accounting management services to public and private organizations in commercial markets throughout the United States.

3rd Position Title

> **Accomplishments**

-
-

Responsibilities

-
-
-
-

4th Position Title

Accomplishments

-
-

Responsibilities

-
-
-
-

EDUCATION

State University of Science and Technology
Master of Science in Computer Engineering
State University of Science and Technology
Bachelor of Science in Engineering Science

INSTRUCTIONAL EXPERIENCE & TRAINING

- **Instructor, Certified XXX:** Preparing candidates for the IT audit exam

- **Adjunct Instructor, County Technical College:**

- **Adjunct Instructor U.S. Military Academy (West Point):** Military science instructor

- **Commander, Army Basic Training:** Life sciences

TECHNOLOGY

Software: Lotus Notes, Open Office, Microsoft Office 2000/XP, Access, Outlook, Word, Excel, PowerPoint and Visio

Programming: C, FORTRAN, ML, LISP, PROLOG, Pascal, BASH, C-Shell, Korn Shell, DOS Command line, PERL, Expect, AWK, BASIC, Assembly, Machine Code (MS) and Ada

Operating Systems: Cisco IOS, Microsoft Server, Windows 2000, XP & Vista; LINUX & XINU, HP-UX, AIX & Solaris, VMWare and MoJoPac

Communications: Wide area, local and wireless networks; fiber optic

Security Tools: Firewalls, code inspection, penetration testing, intrusion detection and prevention, antivirus and spam, Internet filtering, RSA SecurID, CheckPoint, TripWire and Crack

Avoiding Common Interview Mistakes

Your resume was picked up by a recruiter, and you now have an interview. Regardless of whether it is a recession, or a booming market, how do you separate yourself from the pack? What is your plan of attack and story for the interview process?

The first step is to understand where you came from and where you want to go. Recruiters and managers want to see a career progression. They also want to see how concisely you can answer their questions.

Prior to the interview, write a page about each of your jobs, listing your responsibilities and major accomplishments. After you write the information, practice it with anyone who will listen. This will help you to memorize the information, thus increasing your level of confidence for the interview.

Having greater confidence, in turn, will help you to focus on listening to the questions instead of trying to figure out what your next response will be. This will give you an advantage over other candidates. You will be able ask good business questions, thus standing out from the competition.

Preplanning and Preparing for the Interview

You're Interview Pitch

Know your story, know your career progression, know why left each job and know any gaps or red flags in your resume. More important, know your pitch and practice it. You need to be able to answer the questions asked about your history quickly and concisely.

Furthermore, ask questions about the opportunity. This is the only way you are going to create a dialogue and learn more about this potential opportunity. Do not be the person six months down the road that says you did not know the job was going to be like this. Guess what? You didn't know because you did not ask. Therefore, you did not learn enough about the job before you accepted it.

Know your Differentiators and Value

Now that you have crafted your accomplishments and committed your story to memory, you have to identify the value you bring to the organization. You need to put this into concise words so that you can articulate your value during the interview process. You only need a few examples, and most likely, your accomplishments will help prove this value.

By asking questions about the job, the employer will tell you what they are looking for (e.g., "I am looking for a team-oriented person who can be assertive, not aggressive, with our internal clients to help them define their requirements.") You can then take this information and apply it to your background. "Mr. Employer, here is one example of where I had to be diplomatic or assertive in my last position."

Knowing and Defining Your Buyer

Knowing your buyer is not any different than dealing with an internal or external customer. With whom are you meeting? What business challenges are keeping the hiring manager up at night? By knowing your buyer you will obtain critical information that will lay foundation for how you approach each interview. For example, a CEO is worried about profitability and reducing costs. An IT director is worried about employee burnout and getting projects done on time. A human resources professional is worried about finding qualified talent as quickly as possible. I've met a lot of individuals who blindly go into an interview without knowing who they are interviewing with or even the organization itself. If you do not know who you are meeting with, you will be starting the interview at a disadvantage. This will cause you to be less confident, and you will not perform the interview at the top of your game.

Researching the Company and Interviewers

Learning about your potential employer is one of the most important aspects of preparing for an interview. If you get the opportunity to learn the names of your interviewers you should perform an online search by name and company (e.g., "Joel Abraham" AND Recruitment). You might be able to find articles, a list of charities and other information about your interviewer, which might give you an edge over other applicants. You also can use professional social networking sites such as LinkedIn or Xobni to see if they have a profile. If they do, find out what the information tells you about them.

I have used this technique prior to every sales call or interview. If I read an article in which a person was mentioned, for example, I would tell the person about my research and how

I came across the article and that I liked it. (I always add that I am not a stalker.) This extra step has provided me with vital information on the interviewer that has enabled me to build the common ground necessary for a successful relationship. Therefore, *do not* skip this step.

Mirroring and Appearance

Whatever your grooming habits are, you must be well groomed for the interview. If you are a smoker, do not smoke before the interview unless your goal is to smell like an ashtray. Make sure that your cologne or perfume is not too strong. (Men, do not apply the cologne with your right hand so that when you shake hands with the interviewer she or he does not smell like you.) Chew on a breath mint prior to the interview. Finally, on the day of the interview, mirror the interviewer — mirror how fast they walk, talk and shake hands. People like to do business with others who are like them. The Morgan Consulting Group has a great video you can buy on mirroring. It is available at www.morgancg.com. The website also provides training materials for recruiters and job seekers on how to have a successful interview.

Interview Questions

I believe others judge our level of intelligence by the questions we ask. Therefore, it is just as important to interview the employer to make sure the job opportunity is the right one for you. Otherwise, you might end up like the employee who six months down road says, "I didn't agree to do this" or "I didn't know it was going to be like this."

I have categorized the interview questions into two types: impression and business questions.

Impression Questions: These questions typically wake up interviewers increasing their level of energy. If you have hired people in the past, you might have been guilty of asking the same comfortable questions over and over to expedite the interview process and get on with your work day. Impression questions break the monotony of the interview and force the employer or recruiter to focus on you.

Two impression questions I like to ask are:

1. If a headhunter were to recruit you to a competitor, what would be the reasons why you would stay here at ABC Company?

2. Describe how ABD Company separates itself from its competitors to attract the top 20 percent of talent currently available?

Business Questions: Business questions are aimed at seeking information about the company and impact the interviewers. Five questions I like to ask are:

1. Is there a variance between where you are now and where you would like to be for this position (or business)?

2. Describe for me what makes a successful [Position, Title or Employee] for ABC Company?

3. What are ABC's strategic goals for the next 12 months? How does that affect you? How does that affect the department? Who else does this affect?

4. What were the successful attributes of the person who had this job before? Where did they fall short?

5. What do you see as the peaks and valleys for ABC Company in the market, and what strategies do you have in place to smooth out those valleys?

Common Interview Mistakes

Issues Recruiters and Hiring Managers Are Facing Right Now

Some of the issues recruiters are experiencing in today's job market would blow your mind. I cannot tell you how many resumes I have read that are prefabricated. (This, of course, is grounds for immediate disqualification.) We also are coming across many unscrupulous candidates who get someone more skilled in their field to participate in the phone interview. I have also heard horror stories from clients who interview the candidate they thought was perfect for the job, and what shows up on the first day is an employee who cannot perform as expected. Similarly, many candidates are providing fake information on social networking sites, such as LinkedIn, by getting others to write excellent reviews for them.

Why am I sharing this? So that you know that recruiters and hiring managers are now skeptical of everyone they interview and are extra careful when performing background checks. This is also translating into tougher interview questions for candidates.

As a result, never embellish or lie in your resume. I have interviewed countless candidates who claim to have knowledge in certain areas. However, when I ask them questions, their expertise consisted of sitting next to someone who did the actual work, or used the software. In an employment downturn, employers are going to go line-by-line on your resume to see what you have actually done. The result is not to catch you in a lie, but to find out what value you can bring to the company or project. If you get caught with credibility issues during the interview, your chances of being considered for the job are reduced to zero percent.

Addressing Red Flags in Your Background

A red flag is something in your resume that strikes the employer as odd, unclear or inappropriate. The most common red flags are gaps in employment, terminations and short-job durations. The key in this area is to identify your red flags and be able to explain concisely and honestly the details in these areas. If you can answer clearly and concisely, the interviewer is more likely to go on to the next question. If you are fumbling around as you respond, the interviewer will become skeptical and might probe your wounds further.

If you have been unemployed for more than year, you need to explain what you have been doing to find a job. If you are able to share your plan and the effort you have put into finding a job, then the employer will wonder less about your candidacy and whether there is something wrong with your attitude.

Also, if you have legal issues, you must be honest in your application or when answering any questions during the interview. Most recruiters and companies understand mistakes happen in life and will look past them if you are honest. If they do not, then that is not the right place for you.

Don't forget to perform an online search on your name to see what information is out there on the Web about you. You can simply write, for example, "Joel Abraham" AND IL OR Recruitment" in the search box to see what comes up. This is important as the recruiter or employer will probably do a search to obtain information on you. You also should search the interviewer to see if they were quoted on any articles, as explained earlier.

Finally, make sure you have dependable references of past managers who can add credibility to your work history if called upon. This is important because, in most cases, companies may have one to three interviews with you, and the final step is to call your references to verify that what you said is true.

The Dreaded Salary Question

Let's face it. The truth of the matter is that you are simply trying not to price yourself out of the opportunity or leave money on the table. However, not sharing your current salary or previous compensation with the recruiter limits your candidacy. Why? First, the company is not sure if it can afford you and will spend more time with candidates that fall into its salary range. Second, not sharing salary information could be misconstrued as a sign that you are difficult to work with or that you have something to hide.

Key: To position yourself for an opportunity so that you do not price yourself out of the job, read the pitch below and practice it:

> "There are two reasons why I am here today. First, money is important. But second, and most important, is opportunity. I see a lot of opportunity here at ABC Company, and because of this opportunity I do not want to price myself out of this position. Therefore, I would entertain your strongest offer."

This response tells the hiring manager that you are willing to take a short-term loss for a long-term gain. If you make it to the offer stage, they know to make you the best offer they can. After the offer is made, the ball is in your court.

The Loaded Interview Question

If the interviewer prefaces a question by describing a program or process challenge make sure to ask who created the program or process and inquire why it was created. Also, ask the interviewer to describe the problem the company is trying to solve through the program or process. In other words, you need to know who created the program *before* you critique it. The interviewee might have thought it was a great idea, and if you slam it, there goes your shot at the job.

Following up After the Interview

Please remember to follow up with a letter or e-mail thanking the prospective employer for their time. I understand that most job seekers are frustrated as they receive little to no feedback from the employer. So, why should you send them something? It's simple: manners and appreciation.

An attitude of gratitude will definitely open new doors for you. I sometimes get cards in the mail thanking me for my time, and I save every single one. Most people do not get mail anymore. It can be a way to truly differentiate you from the competition. My advice: do both. Send an e-mail so the urgency is there and then surprise them with a thank you card or letter. You do not need to spend a lot of money on this the letter.

Summary

Let's recap. Before the interview, remember to do the following five things:

1. Have the proper positive attitude.
2. Properly research the company and position.
3. Rehearse your pitch and job story.
4. Prepare questions to ask the interviewer.
5. Follow up with an e-mail, letter or both.

You are now ready for the interview.

Leverage Your Network to Create Job Opportunities

Before I start explaining different networking strategies to create job opportunities — which I believe is the best way to proactively magnetizing opportunities to you instead of the traditional way of job hunting — I would like to share another story with you.

Every day, I ask job seekers like you what their next steps are when they do not hear back on from a recruiter or employer after applying for a position. The feedback is always the same. I follow up with the last contact I had for the company via e-mail or phone. I then ask them to describe what they do if they still do not hear from the recruiter. The common response, "I stop calling them."

My follow-up question is, "Why?" The typical response I get is that they have no one else to contact. Most job seekers I talk to feel uncomfortable entering the company through nontraditional means. Instead, they apply where the competition is the fiercest — via the traditional method of applying online. However, the traditional way of applying is the choke point for thousands of applicants looking for work for all of the company's positions.

So what should you do the same? Do you remember when

I talked about how to control the future of your career? Controlling your future begins and ends with building your personal and professional network.

During the second economic downturn in 2001, I started throwing Pink Slip Parties in Wisconsin to help proactive employers network with potential candidates. Throughout the year, I helped approximately 55 job seekers find work. Many of these individuals still attended the next event as a way to network, even though they had jobs. Yet, others did not. That year, many people were laid off three to four times due to the tough economic climate. Regular attendees who kept networking found jobs right away, while the others who stopped networking had to start all over again.

The moral of this story is that those who continued to network got to know employers and employers got to know them. They felt comfortable with each other and, as a result, it was easier for the recruiters to recommend these individuals. The hiring process can be quite scary, so the better you get to know the company and the recruiter, the more prepared you will be to make an educated decision. Let's face it, many hiring managers in the United States consider if they like you first, then whether you can do the job.

The best job search strategy is to develop business networks — associations that fit with your background and the industry that you are trying to get into. Also, do not forget charitable groups, as there are a lot of companies that want their employees, managers and executives to give back to the community.

In today's business climate controlling your future begins and ends with developing and building personal and professional networks. Many people give me excuses for not building a social network, "I do not have time" or "I have too many family commitments." My response to them is that you have to make the time. This is a commitment for your personal and professional future. Unfortunately, people are learning this lesson the hard way. Now I am seeing people rush to catch up out of desperation or survival instinct through online resources. If this if you, I urge to pause and reevaluate your process.

Social Networking

Taking an Inventory of Your Connections

What connections do you have? Look at who you know, what social networking groups do you, or you should, belong to and what religious or charitable groups are you associated with.

Organize Contacts

Organize contacts in order of importance to your career. Find the contacts with the most influential network that can be strategically leveraged to your benefit.

Prioritize Connections

Define your message and who or what communication gets sent to your prioritized contacts:

1. Primary: Top-Tier Business, Family and Social Networks (e.g., LinkedIn and Facebook).

2. Secondary: Family and Friends, Other Business Contacts.

3. Tertiary: Religious Institutions, Charities.

4. Undefined: Transactional Networking.

Make a Communications Plan

How do you get the word out to get help or get the word out about your situation, needs and skills? For example:

- Who do I contact first if I lose my job or if I fear losing my job? Who do I contact second or third?

- How do I stay in touch with from my contacts and how (e.g., phone, e-mail or face-to-face)?

Technology Tools to Stay Organized

How to Craft Search Strings to Find Jobs Quicker: Boolean searches allow you to combine words and phrases using the words AND, OR, NOT and NEAR (otherwise known as Boolean operators) to limit, widen or define your search. Most Internet search engines, and Web directories, default to these Boolean search parameters anyway, but a good Web searcher should know how to use basic Boolean operators.

Definition of Boolean Search Operators:[1]

- The Boolean search operator AND is equal to the "+" symbol.

- The Boolean search operator NOT is equal to the "-" symbol.

- The Boolean search operator OR is the default setting of any search engine (i.e., all search engines will return all the words you type in, automatically).

- The Boolean search operator NEAR is equal to putting a search query in quotes (i.e., "Spongebob Squarepants").

---

1   Source: About.com, "Boolean Search — What Does Boolean Search Mean?" by Wendy Boswell

You are essentially telling the search engine that you want all of these words in this specific order or this specific phrase.

Job Board Aggregators:

Job board aggregates compile listings from thousands of websites, including job boards, newspapers, associations and company career pages. Job seekers do not apply for jobs through the job aggregator site. They simply receive a listing indicating where the job is posted. Applicants can then decide which jobs are of interest and go to the corresponding sites to apply.

The top three job board aggregators are:

1. Indeed.com.
2. Simplyhired.com.
3. Jobster.com.

Professional and Business Networks

Three main types of professional and business networks exist. These are personal blogs, corporate and organization blogs and blog search engines. Following is a brief definition of each to get your acquainted with their functionality.[2]

Personal Blogs: The personal blog, an ongoing diary or commentary by an individual, is the traditional, most common blog. Personal bloggers usually take pride in their blog posts even if their blog is never read. Blogs often become more than a way to just communicate — they become a way to reflect on life or works of art.

Blogging can have a sentimental quality. Few personal blogs

---

2   Source: Wikipedia

rise to fame and the mainstream, but some personal blogs quickly garner an extensive following. One type of personal blog, referred to as a microblog, is extremely detailed and seeks to capture a moment in time. Some sites, such as Twitter, allow bloggers to share thoughts and feelings instantaneously with friends and family.

Corporate and Organizational Blogs: A blog can be private, as in most cases, or it can be created for business purposes. Blogs used internally to enhance the communication and culture in a corporation or externally for marketing, branding or public relations purposes are called corporate blogs. Similar blogs for clubs and societies are called club blogs, group blogs or by similar names. Their purpose is to inform members and other interested parties of club and membership-related activities.

Blog Search Engines: Several blog search engines are used to search blog contents, such as Technorati, Bloglines and BlogScope. Technorati is among the most popular blog search engines and provides current information on popular searches and tags used to categorize blog postings.

Twitter: Twitter is a social networking and microblogging service that enables its users to send and read messages known as *tweets*. Tweets are text-based posts of up to 140 characters displayed on the author's profile page and delivered to the author's subscribers known as *followers*. Senders can restrict delivery to those in their circle of friends or, by default, allow open access. Since late 2009, users can follow lists of authors instead of following individual authors. All users can send and receive tweets via the Twitter website, short message service (SMS) or external applications such as those developed for smartphones.

Social Networking Etiquette

Before you start participating in a social networking site, keep the following points in mind:

- Do not promote only yourself without regard for those around you.

- Complete your profile with accurate information about you and your business. Use your real name and your own photo. Pick a screen name that represents you and your company well. Don't call yourself "Lovebug" unless you want to be known by that name. Also, although your pet may be adorable, do not include a picture of your dog or cat unless you specialize in pet care.

- Offer information of value. Refrain from just talking about yourself and your company. Succinctly write interesting and timely information that will be of benefit to others.

- Do not approach strangers and ask them to be friends to try to sell them on your talents, ideas, products or services. You will quickly lose credibility.

- Do not send requests for invitations to play online games, take personality tests or other timewasters for those using the site.

- Avoid putting anything on the Internet that you don't want your boss, future boss, current client or potential clients to read.

- If someone does not want to be your friend, accept it gracefully. They have the right to make that decision and you must accept it.

- Never post when you are exhausted, inebriated, jet-lagged, angry or upset.

- Do not over-post or over tweet. Your audience will become tired of you; your information may not be taken seriously or even be skipped.

LinkedIn Etiquette Tips

The following list represents 25 actions users of LinkedIn typically perform that hinder their efforts at networking effectively with other professionals:

LINKEDIN RECOMMENDATIONS

1. Asking for a recommendation from someone that you do not personally know nor have never worked together with.

2. People getting or giving recommendations to family members to boost up their numbers.

3. People who, after giving them a recommendation, won't respond to your request for one.

4. Someone asking for a recommendation out of the blue despite being out of contact for several years.

LINKEDIN INVITATIONS

5. Receiving invitations from strangers without a personalized text or reason to connect.

6. Cold-calling salespeople who send you invitations.

LINKEDIN MESSAGES

7. Spam. One person remarked, "The amount of SPAM I am receiving is drowning out the quality of discussions and information others have taken the

time to post here. I have stopped receiving most updates from groups and cancelled membership in others that are filled with it."

8. Being added to a mailing list simply because you are connected with someone.

9. People that don't respond after contacting them.

LINKEDIN STATUS UPDATES

10. People who use their Status Update to "tweet." (There is Twitter for that!).

LINKEDIN INTRODUCTIONS

11. Recruiters who want Introductions but don't give introductions (i.e., they join a social network, yet choose not to be sociable).

LINKEDIN ANSWERS

12. Posting banal questions that are more like ice breakers at a social event. For example, how do you define success? What do you love about LinkedIn? What do you hate about LinkedIn? Do you tweet?

13. People who post a question and then answer their own question with their advertising.

LINKEDIN GROUPS

14. LinkedIn group discussion board spam. "There should be more active moderation of all groups, such spam should be deleted and users who abuse their membership should be blocked or banned."

15. Hardcore, unsophisticated sales pitches in the group discussion or status sections.

16. Rock fights in open forums. If you have an issue with somebody, take it outside then throw down.

17. Job advertisements not posted on the LinkedIn group jobs boards.

18. Members of LinkedIn groups who clearly don't belong in the groups.

19. People who join groups solely to self promote and never exchange ideas or contribute to the group.

20. Posting a link in the group discussions boards in the headline instead of the text area. Links put in the headline cannot be directly clicked and it forces the reader to cut and paste the URL into their browser.

21. People whose comments on discussions or questions have little value.

22. People that post "please hire me" on group discussion boards.

23. Jobs or comments posted in groups without indication of what city or country they are located in.

24. Group spam, despite the fact that settings were supposed to prevent that from happening.

25. Responses to posts that have no relation to the group discussion or question.

One Final Point on Social Networking: You will need to define the protocols of who, what, when, where, why and how for each of your groups. Some contacts you can call directly and explain how they can help, while some contacts are needed simply to lend their name and introduce you to their contacts.

Think of it this way. The contacts closest to you are the most influential in directly helping your career path and should be your top priority. Therefore, establishing a pattern of communication with them is critical. The farther out you go from your network, the less amount of time you want to spend reaching out because it is much colder and you do not want to be thought of as a spammer.

Remember, the further away from the primary contact list you go, the more critical it is that you evaluate each contact, and try to set up some communication with the person. You never know how he or she could help, or who could turn into your next primary network contact.

Key: By now you are starting to feel good about creating a communication plan that will allow you to use your top critical contacts to get the word out for you. However, you need to check the health of your network. It is important to reach out to your network to see how everyone is doing. You need to make a plan and decide who and what the frequency of your contacts will be. You do not want to be a pest, but at the same time you do not want your networks to think that you only call when you need something.

Leveraging Your Network

Magnetize Opportunities

If you get nowhere with the company's website or human resources department, find a close contact within the company and network with the person. Don't start talking about the job right off the bat; rather, reach out to the person to understand the organization better, in particular what they do and what the company is like. Tell them you are impressed with what you learned and saw that there is a job posting for which you feel you are a great fit. Then ask your contact to look at your background and give you an opinion. If they agree you are a good fit, ask your contact if he or she would forward it to the appropriate person. Some companies pay referral fees to their employees.

Arranging Appointments

While different social networking sites exist, the technique below applies to all of them. To keep this simple, I will use LinkedIn as an example to walk you through the process of what has been successful for me and other job seekers.

Earlier, I asked you to take stock of your contacts and prioritize your social network in order of importance starting with your most influential connections. Now it is time to reach out and build a relationship with these individuals.

First, please let me lay the backdrop for those who have not used LinkedIn, or may just be starting to use this website. LinkedIn organizes connections by degrees closest to you. When you connect directly with someone, he or she will be your first line connection. You will get exposure to that person's connections, which will be second line of connection. Why is this important? This is going to frame out how you reach and connect to other people on LinkedIn. Obviously, the closer the connection is to you, the more credibility you have in getting the second or third tier contact to link up with you.

Several methods and strategies exist for reaching out to connections on LinkedIn to which you want to connect. How you will apply your strategy will depend on how you want to manage and organize your connections.

Direct Invitation to Connect

LinkedIn members can only connect through invitations. For two people to connect on LinkedIn one must invite the other, and the other must accept the invitation. If the person being invited is not a member of LinkedIn, he or she will need to join to accept the invitation. For more information, go to the LinkedIn help section and type "sending invitations to connect."

Important to know: depending on your account type (i.e., free or premium), you will be allowed a certain amount of direct connections per month. Also, there are a maximum number of connections you can use, 3,000. Once you have gone over that limit, you need to contact customer services.

Similarly, if four or more people say that they do not know you, your account will be frozen and you will have to contact customer services to unfreeze your account. Most people do not realize that by saying you do not know the person sending you the invitation; you might be freezing an account.

If someone sends me an invitation I prefer not to connect with, or I'm unsure about, I archive that connection so it does not harm the individual. Also, I add this wording to all of my connections and InMails to cut down on the number of individuals indicating that they do not know me.

> "Please review my profile before you decide to accept or decline my invitation. I would like for you to see that I am legitimate, and if you decide to decline my invitation please archive it just in case you would like to accept it i the future."

InMail

InMail allows you to send messages directly to LinkedIn users you couldn't reach otherwise. It allows you to contact or to be directly contacted by second or third degree contacts, as well as LinkedIn users who are not in your network. It is not necessary to send InMails to members who are first degree connections or members of the same group. You can communicate directly with these connections at no cost by using the "Send Message" link in the upper right area of the member's Profile.

Key: depending on your account type (i.e., free or premium), you only have a certain amount of InMails per month. Another important factor is your InMail feedback score. It is important to customize your message so that the person receiving it can see that you are a legitimate networker and not someone trying to send spam or, worse, a scammer. I include the message below in all of my Inmails:

> "Please review my profile before you decide to accept or decline my invitation. I would like for you to see that I am legitimate and if you decide to decline my invitation, please archive my information just in case you would like to accept it in the future. If you are interested please respond to this in mail and I will send you an invitation."

Joining a Group and Communicating Through InMail

First-degree connections can contact you directly by sending a LinkedIn message, and you can be contacted by anyone in your network through an Introduction. In addition, second and third degree contacts outside of your network can contact you directly through InMail. Premium account holders can also choose to accept OpenLink messages from any LinkedIn user.

Changing Your Contact Messages

For those who do not have a premium account you are going to get the biggest bang for your buck by networking with members in your group. You can send an InMail for free. But, again, the credibility of your message and feedback score is important.

Working Your Network

Let's recap. You organized your network in order of importance. You took stock in your first-tier contacts. What happens next? Now it's time to go out and network.

The first thing that I do is look at the connections of my first-tier contacts to see if there are any people I feel I have something in common with. I then reach out to these contacts to build my network so I have access to more contacts. Remember, there is no reason to spam everyone on LinkedIn. You will come across individuals with thousands of contacts. Once you reach more than a couple hundred contacts, you will be unable to effectively manage your connections or provide value to your contacts. Value equals more opportunity for you.

Tip: Remember your LinkedIn etiquette. All of your messages should be customized to separate you from the competition. See the LinkedIn example below. I recommend that you do not use this same exact message as others might do this. Rather, create your own similar message.

Name Hi,

I saw your profile in LinkedIn and was impressed with your background. I would like to start networking with you to get a better understanding of what trends you are seeing in the X industry and Y market. I am networking with other decision makers across the United States. As you will see that you and I share a few common connections. In return for networking, I can be tapped at any time to share with you the insights and experience from my other contacts.

Please review my profile before you decide to accept or decline my invitation. I would like for you to see that I am legitimate, and if you decide to decline my invitation please archive my information just in case you would like to accept it in the future. If you are interested, please respond to this in mail and I will send you an invite.

Thank you again for all of your time and I look forward to sharing my network with you.

Joel Abraham E-mail
Cell phone number

Three things are going to happen after sending an invitation to connect to someone. If you monitor your sent box in LinkedIn you will see the progress of your message (i.e., In Progress or Sent, Accepted, Don't Know or Expired).

Acceptance

First, you are going to get responses from people who want to connect with you. The next step is for you to develop a compelling reason to set up a time to talk live. The conversation should focus on what you have in common and what you can offer your contact (i.e., access to your contacts who in turn can help them do their job better.) You know your industry best. Make sure that you are prepared before you reach out again by thanking them for connecting and asking to set up a phone or face-to-face meeting.

Don't Know

Do not worry if you receive this response. Simply review the message you sent and try to determine how it have been interpreted by the contact. Was this the right message for this person? Was this connection a risk I wanted to take because we had nothing in common? If all else fails, call the company and ask for the person to network with you. Do not ask the individual why he indicated that he didn't know you. You will be perceived as a stalker or, worse, crazy. In addition, you will get yourself blackballed from networking.

Finally, after you call the individual ask her if it is a good time to talk. I have received many calls in the past where the person has not respected my time and started talking to me right away. Unfortunately, we weren't even on the same page.

If you have one shot at talking to someone, you want to make sure that you have the person's attention and that she is not doing something else.

Nothing

Please keep in mind that communication through LinkedIn is fluid — it is unlike for everyone to check the website every five minutes. Therefore, you are going to have to be patient and watch your sent box to monitor the progress of your messages.

InMail Follow-up

Following up with your connections is key. We took different approaches for connecting. First, we identified actionable next steps for the people with whom we connected. Second, we took our list and stripped it from the website to connect with more professionals via LinkedIn. The final step is setting up appointments with our new contacts.

Actionable Next Steps

While you are networking via phone or e-mail, you need to understand what level or type of connections your new contact would find beneficial. This will allow you to hunt a quality contact to share with your new connection. This, in turn, will result in a second reason to follow up with them. Identifying a contact for them is critical in keeping the relationship moving forward.

Here is an example that I experienced recently. I am connected to someone who was looking to create an Enterprise IT Governance Strategy. He then asked me if I knew anyone who had experience in creating this type of strategy. I quickly went to my network, found two high-level connections and contacted them asking if they would be interested in networking. I now had something important to help my targeted contact do his job better. More important, I had given him something before I asked for anything in return.

Once you introduce someone, remember to mark your calendar to follow up with the individuals to determine if the introductions were of any value or if they need more support.

Also, be smart about asking for something in return. Timing is everything. If you do help someone wait a day or two before you ask for something back, unless your contact offered to help you. Make sure you keep track of everything so that you can stay organized. Sometimes it takes a while to find the right connection for the type of contact you are targeting.

Finally, take a step back and look at what just happened.

> You targeted and met a new contact →
> That contact needed some guidance →
> You leveraged your contact to find someone who could help →
> The individual you introduced to your contact felt great that you thought of him and introduced her to a new contact →
> And, all of this happened without asking for anything in return =
> You created value for your network and created credibility for yourself.

This process applies to any social networking situation. Remember to ask for an invitation to join a person's network if the dialogue occurs via InMail.

Phone or Face-to-Face Interview

This is the most critical step of the social engineering process as this is the first step in building a long-term relationship that will be the catalyst for magnetizing opportunities to you. For most people I talk to, the live contact is the most challenging thing to them. I understand that for most people this can be uncomfortable or even somewhat unnatural. Regardless, setting up a live contact creates an actionable event for you to start networking and providing value. More important, a live contact helps leverage the new relationship so that you can land the job at a company you have had no feedback from. Next I will share with you tactics and approaches to making this critical step easier.

I am going to first break this down into three basic thought processes:

1. Setting the stage of how to network to take the mystery out of your live conversation.

2. Networking with influencers.

3. Networking with targeted decision makers working in organizations where you have found job opportunities, whether you have applied and have not received a response or simply want to attack this opportunity from the top down.

The assumption that I am going to make is that you are connected to the person on a social network. Therefore, this should be a much warmer call instead of a cold call, as you are connected with the individual, and there is an immediate bond whether he remembers you or not. Try to keep the date you connected to the person handy so that he can search his e-mail. This helps to legitimize your connection.

Key: remember to ask if it is a good time to talk and how much time she can give you. If you only get one shot to network with someone you need to make sure the person is not distracted. Finally, before you get off the phone ask her how she wants to communicate moving forward (i.e., phone or e-mail) and the frequency of communication. You do not want your connections to dread your calls or view you as a stalker.

1. **Setting the Stage.**

During the past seven years, whenever I contact someone I met via LinkedIn and the person realizes that I am a headhunter or in sales, the person typically feels uncomfortable about my call. Therefore, at the beginning, my efforts were not good at building a solid relationship. I finally got frustrated and asked one of the IT directors what I could have done differently after our conversation. She said that at first she was confused on why I was calling, which made her feel apprehensive when we started talking. She then recommended that I should set the stage on how and why people should network with me. This was my "Aha!" moment.

So now when I talk to people, I ask them if it is okay for me to take the mystery out of our networking call by sharing with them how others use me to network. My pitch sound like this:

> "I have been networking with people for more than six years and have that others want to network with me for three reasons. Some of these reasons can be blended together or just for a single purpose. First, people use me to help them improve their job performance by using my network to help them find industry connections that they can brainstorm with on issues, challenges and ideas. The second area that people use me for is to help them find IT security contractors to

help with their human capital challenges. And the last area is for them to get job advice or need help finding a new career."

I then ask them how they would like to network with me. This has always started the conversation on a positive note.

Key: Remember the type of value you bring to a connection so that people can network with you more effectively. To do so, create a spreadsheet so that you can keep track of what is important to each connection. I am a firm believer that if someone needs a connection you should try and find one in your network or seek one out right away. It is easy to drop the ball on this if you are not organized. Also, if you are able to deliver a connection to the individual, you will have done two things. First, you build credibility. Second, you have given the person something before you ask for anything in return. This, in my opinion, gives you the right to ask for something in return when you need it.

2. Networking With Influencers.

This call is a much easier one to make since you will be calling people from your same industry. Therefore, you have a lot more in common and can talk about trends, common challenges or business issues. However, your objective here is to find out what connections you have that will help them and be able to share what type of connections you are looking for. These contacts are who you will be farming and cultivating to bring in opportunities. Remember these connections will take a lot of work to cultivate — so it is a marathon and not a short race.

3. Networking With Targeted Decision Makers

One item to keep in mind to have a successful conversation is that you will need to find a commonality first. In your first contact you should not be asking the person to submit your resume for the job posting you have seen or applied. That is self-serving, and you have not built up any credibility with the person yet. Finding common ground could sharing the same experiences the two of you have or networking about trends in the profession, talking about the school you both attended or the same groups you belong to.

That is what your first dialogue should be about. I know that the market is competitive and time is not your friend, but you are going to have to be patient and wait a few days before you reach out back to the person.

After your first contact, you need to find a reason to reach out to the person again. At this point, I conduct research on the company or person. For instance, when you make the second call you can compliment the person by letting her know that you were so impressed with your previous conversation that you wanted to learn more about the company. While you were doing research on the organization, you saw that a vacant position was available for which you believe you are a potential fit and wanted to call to learn more about the company culture before you apply.

If your dialog is positive, I would then ask if she can recommend anyone you could submit your resume too or if she would be willing to send it to the right person. Remember some companies have referral bonuses for employees who refer candidates who get hired.

Improving Your Performance and Message

After every successful or unsuccessful networking experience you need to stop and reflect on the event. You need to ask, "What could I do differently? How can I improve my message?

What was I able to get out of this conversation that will lead me to a second or third conversation or even a new contact?

Blogging and Networking Don'ts

With social media becoming part of our daily lives it is important for you to remember not to talk negatively about the company at which you just interviewed. Recently, I had a candidate tell me that she lost a job opportunity she was overqualified for because she posted on her blog that the person who interviewed her was clueless and she was certain she landed the job. Little did she know the hiring manager did an online search and read her post. The manager called her the next day to tell her that she would have had the job, but her candidacy was retired after he read her comments on the company and him. He told her that her comments were unprofessional and that he thought it was an important lesson for her to learn that anything posted on the Internet is public.

My mom always told me that lose lips sink ships. This is true. Many people I am helping blind copy me and others on their job search updates and connections. I know people are excited and want to share their progress. However, the amount of information freely share about these opportunities — from the job position and description to the contacts — can be used against them. For instance, what if this information should fall into the wrong hands, such as another job seeker? Therefore, whenever you are blogging or posting a comment on Facebook or LinkedIn, choose the information you would like to share wisely so as not to increase your competition for the coveted positions you have uncovered.

Your Mental State

On a daily basis when I talk to candidates, I ask them how their job search is going. The response I typically get is peaks and valleys. I ask if there participated in any interviews for which they did not get the job and, if so, why they feel they did not get the job. I know I am opening a Pandora's Box by asking this question, but I am testing the candidates' state of mind. Are they desperate? What is their attitude about the job search?

All of a sudden the flood gates open up, and I start hearing things such as, "I was overqualified," "I am too old" or "I am too expensive." By then, frustration or depression rears its ugly head. I ask them how they know this information: "Have you talked to the human resources contact or the hiring manager?" The respond is always, "No."

Let me set something straight right now. When this happens to you, which I know is disappointing, do not beat yourself up with negative thoughts. Especially since, in reality, you have no idea as to whether they are true or not. If you get that type of feedback from a recruiter or hiring manager, then you can come up with solutions. However, if you do not know why you weren't contacted, then you are wasting your precious energy on negative thoughts rather than focusing your time on more fruitful events.

One of the biggest job searching challenges that you are going to face is keeping your emotions in balance. You are going to be dealing with hiring managers, human resources personnel, recruiters and even procurement agents who are going to qualify you for the position. All of a sudden, you will get a lot of activity with companies for which you would be excited to work. You are sure that they need your skills and would like to hire you because you are a high performer. Furthermore, your accomplishments made a difference on the return on investment of your previous employer. In fact, you are such a great candidate you have three or four opportunities lined up. Things are great so you tell your significant other, your friends or even past associates.

Then next day you do not hear a thing. No one gets back to you. No one has the stones to tell why you did not get for the job. No one tells you why you did not get even a shot at any opportunity in the company. All you remember is that you were told, "I like your style," or "Your accomplishments would fit right into what we need here at ABC Company."

All you are left with are questions such as, "What is wrong with me?" "Could I have done anything differently?" "What am I going to say to my family or friends who keep asking me how my search is going?" "Why does this happen to me?" "How am I going to take care of my responsibilities?"

STOP

You are not alone. This happens to all of us. The "why" is due to most companies recruiting for what their needs are now, not what their needs will be in the future. That is why as soon as the company or agency finds the right company everything drops. You are no longer a priority. Right or wrong, that's how things work.

As a manager, think back on how relieved you were when you had a critical opening or need that was filled. When was the last time you thought of the second or third place candidate? What was communicated to them? I don't feel hiring managers are trying to be mean-spirited, hurtful or malicious. However, they are short sited. Either way, you shouldn't take this personally. There is nothing wrong with you.

Rules for Job Search Sanity

1. Keep your emotions in check. If people ask how the job search is going, just smile and say, "It's in progress."

2. You are looking for the right opportunity and companies are looking for the right employee. The interview or screening needs to go two ways. I am a firm believer that what separates us from others is our ability to ask intelligent questions. So know your story. Know where you came from and where you want to go, so that you can listen to what is being asked. Answer concisely and quickly. Know the company or environment so that you can ask intelligent questions to determine if this is the right company for you.

3. For every $10,000 you would like to earn, add one month to your search. Prepare yourself mentally that it could take a long time for you to find the right opportunity. If you were a director or vice president, there are not a lot of positions floating around and most likely you were making more than $40,000 a year. Therefore, be patient. If you need money immediately, talk to a contracting or staffing agency

to find a source of temporary income while you find a better, more permanent opportunity.

4. Run your job search like your own business. You need to manage your contacts, interviews, thank-you letters and resume submittals like a sales person. You need to identify which contacts and companies you want to keep in touch with and which websites you will visit in search for opportunities on an ongoing basis. I would not rely on the company or recruiter to remember you for other opportunities. The people who stay top of mind get the first opportunities. However, you do not want to be a stalker. You need to find out how they prefer to be contacted.

5. Keep networking even after you land your job. In a current market like this, you could potentially be laid off more than once. Also, you need to "pay forward" the kindness you received from other people who helped you in the first place.

New Certification or Training: Should I Invest in Myself?

Over the past holiday season and into 2011, I have been contacted with more frequency by many IT decision makers looking for information on current employment trends and career path advice. Most people I have been talking to are being proactive and looking to improve their technical and business skills. These professionals are committed to continuing their education, certifications and other training to protect their future and provide career stability for their families.

Before you decide to invest in a new college degree, certification or training, you need to decide whether doing so is a wise financial decision. For example, will getting a new certification improve your professional or technical skills? If you are working on a certification or degree, finish what you started. I am a firm believer that a short-term loss for a long-term gain is a good investment to make.

However, do be practical and use common sense in your career path strategy. If a brand new certification comes out, and you are not sure whether the investment is worthwhile, ask yourself, "Is the financial investment or risk worth the reward? Are job seekers being rewarded right now for these skills?"

To answer these questions monitor different job boards and look for any demand on that certification or the technical skill you are looking to acquire for your industry. (Indeed.com provides great information and real-time keyword trends you can search by.) Doing a search will enable you to stay ahead of the curve and help you decide whether you need to make the investment.

If you decide you need the degree, certification or new training, go for it; if you are still unsure, save your money.

Finally, you need to monitor the job boards, user groups, and social networks such as LinkedIn to check the pulse of what is going on in your market. If you are concerned that you are not going to be as competitive, you should leverage your network to see what their employers need currently or will need in the future. For instance, you might read in a job posting that the skill or certification is "nice to have" (i.e., its costs more). Next, you will read it is a "requirement" (i.e., there is increased market value in that skill). Therefore, whenever you identify several "nice to have," this is a sigh that you could move forward or find another investment in yourself.

Common Sense Is Not Common

Although many would find the following pieces of advice to be commonsensical, they are worth stating in the likelihood that you might be one of those individuals who have never given any of the recommendations below any thought:

- Dress to impress, no matter the environment.

- Get a haircut if you can before the interview. Do not, however, wait for the day of the interview to get a haircut. I went to get an emergency haircut before an interview at one of those cheap and fast hair salons. I then went to my interview without giving my new hairdo much thought. When I got home my wife laughed at me. One side burn was one-inch longer than the other. Needless to say I did not get the job.

- If you put cologne or perfume use your left hand no one wants to leave an interview smelling like the person they just met.

- If you smoke, do not smoke a pack of cigarettes before you go in for your interview.

- Do not smoke during a phone interview either. I have heard many people smoke while they are talking to me over the phone. That is not professional.

- Remember to research the company you are interviewing with as well as the interviewers if you can.

- Focus on the things that are important to the company you are interviewing for:

- The result the company is looking for.

- Any evidence you can give on how you can deliver those results.

- A progression track in your previous performance.

- Use action words during the interview: planned, created, developed, integrated, originated, initiated, conceived, formulated, etc.

- Similarly, use result-oriented phrases: lead to, contributed to, demonstrated that, provided for, increased the value in, shot holes in, etc.

- Send thank you e-mails and letters. Sending a letter is a great way to differentiate yourself as many don't take the time to send me and people rarely receive them.

Conclusion

I estimate that the average professional candidate voluntarily spends more than $1,000 worth of their own time and money preparing for and participating in an organization's hiring process. Given that level of investment, they deserve to be treated like good customers. Dr. John Sullivan, "How Candidate Abuse Is Costing Your Firm Millions of Dollars in Revenue"

One thousand dollars seems incredibly low to me, especially if you consider that the average person is unemployed for approximately nine months plus. However, I think the information Dr. John Sullivan cites typifies how much effort, investment and time your competition is putting forth to find and land their desired job. This is not a guideline for what you should spend looking for a job, but should serve as a reality check of who you are competing against.

In summary, most of the people I talk to are using the traditional way of job hunting (i.e., posting a resume and waiting for a call). The results they are getting are abysmal — the job "black hole" of frustration due to the lack of feedback, no clear steps on how to proceed or lack of closure after an interview. This is the reason why I wrote this book — to help you break through that job "black hole" by giving you actionable techniques and strategies to liberate yourself from the waiting game.

I firmly believe that the tips in this book will help you build a sustainable network, bring new opportunities to you, give you a positive attitude and increase your confidence, thus providing you with the desired job opportunity in a shorter amount of time than the traditional way of job hunting.

This process has been a humbling experience for me and it is with great gratitude that I am able to share with you the experiences I have acquired for the last 17 years. Every day I share this information in an effort to inspire as many people I can.

Thank you for taking the time to read this. I hope you are able to at least find one, two or several tips useful in helping you gain back your competitive edge. I am confident when you add these techniques together and put in the effort; you will not only achieve your short-term goals of finding a job, but will help liberate yourself from the traditional job hunting process. You will have created the tools and cultivated a long-term network that will bring opportunities to you.

One final thought I want to recap is that this is marathon and not a short-term race. Applying the techniques in this book will take time. However, if you put forth the effort you will be successful. I am living proof their success — I have used them and made it through three economic recessions.

Thank you again for your time. I believe in you, and now you need to believe in yourself and remember it is a marathon not a sprint!

"Success is the sum of small efforts, repeated day in and day out".

Robert Collier